MARIA BENNETTI

NOW AND TEN

A guide to reclaiming the joy
that's always been yours

Now And Ten

A guide to reclaiming the joy that's always been yours

Published By Platypus Publishing

Copyright © 2025 Maria Bennetti

All rights reserved. No portion of this book may be reproduced in any form without permission from the publisher, except as permitted by U.S. copyright law.

Printed in The United States

Paperback Edition

ISBN: 978-1-968253-08-0

For Matt, Lucas and Nico

Thanks for making finding joy
in life so easy

CONTENTS

Introduction		9
Chapter 1:	Let's Get Into It	12
Chapter 2:	The Magic of Being Ten	16
Chapter 3:	Why It Was Easy Then (and Why It's Hard Now)	22
Chapter 4:	The Science of Joy	34
Chapter 5:	Play Isn't Just for Kids	45
Chapter 6:	Reconnecting with Your 10-Year-Old Self	54
Chapter 7:	Missteps on the Road to Joy	64
Chapter 8:	Making Joy a Habit	73
Chapter 9:	The Joy of Connection	80
Chapter 10:	Living a Life Guided by Joy	87

INTRODUCTION

Where did this idea come from?

Basically, Twenty-five years in hospitality and a growing awareness of how much we rely on manufactured joy as adults.

I started in the service industry in college, working the early shift at a coffee shop in Manhattan Beach. The 6am crowd was groggy, half-awake, and laser-focused on their caffeine, and there was something surprisingly wonderful about being the person who handed it to them. That first cup, that first sip, it brought real joy to their faces, unfiltered and honest.

Since then, I've worn many hospitality hats: waitress, restaurant manager, wine industry professional, and eventually, winery founder. Over the last three decades, I watched the wine world shift, especially in the direct-to-consumer space. In the early days, tasting rooms were casual and authentic: a modest tasting fee, a branded glass as a free souvenir, and usually the winemaker behind the bar pouring tastes, telling you about the vines, the vintage, and the story behind the bottle. It was personal and grounded. The focus was on the wine and creating a meaningful connection with the guest.

Today, the winetasting consumer is met with a myriad of choices, ranging from reserve cave tours, artful food pairings, ziplining over the vineyards, and much, much more. And while all of that can be exciting, it's also a show; an expensive, highly curated experience where the wine now plays second fiddle. That soulful, simple connection? It's been replaced by wow-factor.

Witnessing this change got me thinking, not just about the wine industry, but about how adults look for joy in general. We tend to chase happiness through more excitement, more luxury, and more everything. But the manufactured joy we find there rarely lasts, sending us back through the "more loop" for the next dopamine hit. We've gotten so used to looking outside ourselves for joy that we've forgotten where it naturally comes from.

So, *was there ever a time when all that "stuff" didn't matter?* Yup, childhood; when joy was simple and unfiltered. As children, we followed joy from the inside and let curiosity lead the way: skating with friends, reading for hours, and getting lost in imaginary worlds. We weren't trying to impress anyone. We weren't documenting, optimizing, or chasing likes. We followed our instincts and did what felt good, what made us feel alive.

The idea sparked. But was it actually valid? Could looking back at your childhood, remembering the things you truly loved to do, and then weave those pieces into your adult life really make a difference? Could it bring *real* joy, or was I just being sentimental? I was curious enough to find out, so I started experimenting.

This book is the story of that experiment; what I tried, what I discovered, and how it quietly shifted the way I moved through life. Spoiler: it works. And the best part? It doesn't require quitting your job or blowing up your life. As a busy mom, I found that you can engage with this idea in whatever way fits your reality. Whether you dive all in or just dip a toe, the reward is still there. The connection still happens.

I ultimately realized when we revisit those childhood joys, the ones that came naturally, without reward or approval, we unearth something profoundly true to our core; something innate. And when I tapped back into that, bringing it into the present, I started to fill my cup again, not with stuff, noise, or validation, but with something real, satiating, and self-validating.

And suddenly, even my morning cup of coffee felt like enough.

CHAPTER 1:
LET'S GET INTO IT

Remember the summer afternoons when you were a kid that stretched endlessly ahead, full of possibility. There were no schedules, deadlines, or need to measure time against anything but the sun inching across the sky. Maybe the afternoons were spent riding a bike up and down the block, scribbling wild ideas in a notebook, or getting so lost in a game with neighborhood friends that time felt irrelevant.

Joy was effortless in those days. We played without self-consciousness, explored without fear of failure, and created without needing validation. We didn't choose activities because they were productive or had a purpose. We chose them because they made our hearts race, our imaginations soar, and our spirits light up. The joy felt in those moments didn't need a reason. It simply was.

Fast-forward to today.

When was the last time you felt that kind of true joy? Not the quick buzz from buying something new or the brief satisfaction of crossing another task off the to-do list, but the happiness that makes the world disappear. That feeling has become elusive for most of us, hiding beneath a mountain of responsibilities and societal expectations. Joy has been shuffled to the margins of our lives, traded for the mirage of productivity and purpose.

As we grow older, life draws us further and further from the things that make us feel like our genuine selves. We learn from the modern world to prioritize work, goals, and external validation over playing, exploration, and wonder. Hobbies become side hustles to justify their worth or are abandoned altogether due to the lack of hours in a day. Social time morphs into networking. Play, the heart of joy, becomes something we watch children do while we sit on the sidelines, busy adulting. No wonder joy feels out of reach; we've pushed it to the periphery, treating it like a bonus instead of a necessity.

In actuality, engaging in joyful activities fuels resilience, fosters creativity, and strengthens connection, allowing us to move through hard work and sacrifice more easily. But even so, society constantly tells us that joy is an indulgence, a treat we can savor only after earning it. But what if that's wrong? What if joy isn't a privilege but something profoundly essential?

The summer afternoon I had you recall is more than an exercise in pinpointing a nostalgic memory. It's a guide to help remind you what makes you feel alive at your core; a tool that peels back the layers of productivity, perfectionism, and external expectations and uncovers the simple joys that once made life meaningful to you. Reconnecting with our childhood selves isn't about escaping adulthood. It's about relearning how to weave joy into the life you have now on your terms. It's about reclaiming the magic of being ten and creating an adult version where joy isn't an afterthought. Those original ten-year-old sparks of joy haven't gone anywhere; they are simply hiding under the complexities of adult life. They have been buried and forgotten, until now.

Look, I'm not a self-help expert. I didn't write this book to add another chore to your already-packed to-do list, and I didn't write it to make you feel obligated to chase some unattainable idea of happiness. It's simply a tool showing you how to remember and go beneath the layers of obligation and expectation to reconnect with the pure joy that once came naturally. For the past five years, I've made a conscious effort to bring play and joy back into my life, and it's made a huge difference in my daily enjoyment, overall happiness, and lowering my stress level. This feels like a win for someone with a Type A personality, a job, kids, and a house to manage. Am I perfect at it? Absolutely not. Some days are so packed that I barely have a second to breathe. Even then, I've learned to give myself grace. Overall, if the days I have the space to insert my joys outnumber the chaotic ones, I figure I'm at least on the right track.

Through my own trial and error, I've learned that finding joy isn't a one-size-fits-all formula. There's no universal checklist that guarantees happiness. Some people, even experts, swear that getting out in nature will bring you happiness. Others say it's exercise. But what if you don't enjoy working out or being in nature? Should you force yourself to do it because someone says it's the key to happiness? No. Joy is intensely personal; it's not about following someone else's path; my joys may not be your joys, and your joys may not be the next person's. Your joy is about tapping back into what you already discovered made you happy when you were young and untethered and making space for it now.

So let's look back, not to live in the past, but to borrow its wisdom and bring it forward. Let's craft a way to infuse our own personal joys into our everyday lives. Let's make our joys a priority, a way of being, a choice we make every day to live fully, freely, and authentically. Let's take this journey together as we rediscover the magic that's been there all along.

CHAPTER 2: THE MAGIC OF BEING TEN

Ten is the sweet spot. It's that perfect age where independence begins to bloom, yet you're still untouched by the weight of societal expectations. You're discovering the world and yourself with an open heart and boundless curiosity. There's no real fear of failing, worrying about how you're perceived, and no pressure to get it right. You're just in the moment, doing what feels good, exciting, and what feels like you.

At ten, you didn't overthink how you spent your free time. If you wanted to do something, you just did it. You didn't wonder if your experimental potion wasted all the milk in the fridge or if riding your bike in circles was a productive use of your time. You were free. Free to follow your curiosity without asking permission. You didn't need a reason to try something. Your curiosity didn't hinge on results. This was the magic of ten: You didn't judge your joy, audit your wonder, or curate your day to make it look good; you just lived it.

Have you thought about your younger version lately? If

you haven't, take a moment to consider who *you* were at ten years old, what you looked like, where you lived, and most importantly, how you lived. What made you laugh uncontrollably? What held your attention so completely that hours slipped by unnoticed? What made you feel alive, most free? What brought you the most joy? I bet it wasn't expensive, complicated, or tied to fancy gadgets and elaborate plans. It was likely the joy that came from the simplest things.

Building Forts

There's nothing like the thrill of creating your own world; a pile of cushions, a few blankets, and maybe a chair or two could transform any room into a hideout. Forts were more than just structures; they were sanctuaries. They were spaces that belonged entirely to you. You were the architect, the ruler, the dreamer. The building process, a little trial, a little error, and a lot of imagination were all part of the fun.

What if you created an adult version of "building a fort" and carved out a space for yourself in the area of your life where you're the busiest? Maybe you're not erecting a literal fort (though why not?), but it could look like personalizing your desk at work to match your personality. If you're on the road often, set up a moving version of your own space. Prepare your drive with a great playlist, favorite snacks, and a figurine on your dash to keep you company. For anyone who finds themselves the busiest at home, why not designate a space where no work ever gets done, no business talk, no studying, and no making to-do lists? Choose an area and make it feel entirely yours. The adult fort is about creating a physical space that allows you to feel more like yourself.

Exploring Outside

The outdoors felt infinite. It was a place to be wild, run, and get muddy. Every tree, rock, and patch of dirt held the potential for discovery. You weren't trying to get anywhere specific. You explored for the sake of exploring, letting your curiosity guide you. You studied bugs, collected treasures like sticks and leaves, and wandered until it was time to return home.

As adults, we often forget how grounding the outdoors can be with work, technology, and weather keeping us indoors. What if we approached going outside like we did at ten, though? What if we wandered without a destination or agenda on an afternoon we had free, put our phones on silent and paid attention to the crunch of leaves underfoot, or sat and watched the clouds even on a windy day? The world is still full of wonder. We need to slow down and notice it.

Drawing or Doodling

Grabbing a stack of scrap paper, whatever crayons you could find, and drawing. You didn't care if your stick figures were wobbly or your colors stayed inside the lines. You only focused on creating, of putting something on paper that came from your mind. It was a natural expression. It didn't matter if anyone saw it or praised it. It was enough that you made it.

So, why not indulge this imaginative side of you, picking out a drawing pad, pencils, and a set of markers, and try doodling again? Not with the goal of making something impressive but just for the fun of it. Let your hand wander across the page. Play with shapes, lines, and colors. Craft a homemade bookmark for a book you are reading, or design a birthday card for a loved one. During the process, focus on how it makes you feel. There's joy in creating and being creative.

Playing Pretend

Your imagination knew no limits. A broomstick became a sword, a cardboard box turned into a spaceship, and an old towel transformed into a superhero cape. You didn't need fancy costumes, props, or even an audience. The act of pretending, of stepping into another world, was its own reward.

As adults, we tend to stifle that imaginative spark by telling ourselves to grow up and focus on reality. But pretend play isn't just for kids. Imagination is a tool to tap into creativity, find answers, and solve problems using a different perspective. Maybe you use role-playing to build confidence in your career. Practice a big presentation in front of the mirror as if you're a world-famous TED Talk speaker, using exaggerated hand gestures and dramatic pauses, allowing yourself to fully embody the role before stepping into it for real.

Being Part of a Team

As a young child, being part of a team wasn't about trophies, stats, or future scholarships. It was about being in it together, the matching jerseys, the shared chants, and the inside jokes during warm-ups. It was showing up because your friends were there and because you loved how it felt to move your body, to try hard, and to high-five your teammates.

You didn't think about winning as much as you thought about playing. You played hard because it was fun, not because someone was watching. You celebrated small things like finally serving the ball over the net or pulling off a pass you didn't think you could. You cheered just as loud for your teammates as you did for yourself.

What if you brought some of that team spirit back into your adult life? Not the competition or pressure, but the camaraderie, the shared energy, and the collective momentum. You could join a local rec league or gather a few friends to shoot hoops or kick a ball at the park. Or maybe it's not sports at all. Perhaps it could be a creative collective, a coworking group, or a band. It reminds you that you don't have to go it alone and that joy often grows when you share it.

As we age, we tend to complicate things. We evaluate, analyze, and compare, measuring ourselves against some invisible standard. We struggle to do something just for fun. We even stop trying new things because we're worried about being judged. Finding your true joy requires you to tap back into that carefree attitude and give yourself permission to enjoy the ride.

CHAPTER 3:
WHY IT WAS EASY THEN
(AND WHY IT'S HARD NOW)

If you've ever watched kids play, you know that joy comes to them effortlessly. They leap into make-believe worlds using their magic wands from fallen twigs and scurry into their caves made from a sheet they draped over the kitchen chairs. They do this with total abandon, unbothered by doubt and self-awareness. Their laughter is loud, their movements unrestrained, and their ideas endless. They don't stop asking whether their game is worth it or if their creation is good enough. They play.

Now, think about how you approach leisure as an adult. Let's use heading to the beach for the day as an example. Does it come with an exhaustive mental checklist? Is there a goal attached, a measure of productivity or usefulness? If not, do you ever feel guilty for taking that time to do something just for fun? If you're like me, the answer is yes. Somewhere along the way, what was once natural and easy became complicated, layered with judgment, expectations, and the constant pressure to make it count.

At ten, joy was a natural state. It didn't require effort or planning; it was just how we navigated the world. This ease wasn't accidental; it came from how our brains worked and how we approached life at that age. Everything about being ten encouraged a kind of freedom that we often lose sight of as adults, even though we technically have more freedom than we did then.

So why was joy so easy then, and why is it so hard now?

Fear of Failure and Judgement

As kids, we didn't fear failure; we barely recognized it. If your homemade slime was too sticky, you didn't throw your hands up and decide you were terrible at science. You adjusted the mix and kept going. If your paper airplane didn't fly straight, you didn't walk away in defeat. You folded another one, tweaking the wings, testing again and again until one finally soared across the room. Trial and error was part of the fun. The process itself *was* the reward. No overthinking, no second-guessing, just experimenting until something worked.

As we grew older, something shifted. Maybe it was a teacher who criticized your art project, a classmate who laughed when you stumbled during a basketball game or a friend who rolled their eyes when you excitedly shared an idea for an afternoon activity. Little by little, self-consciousness started to grow, and now, as adults, it's practically second nature to question ourselves. *What will people think? Am I good enough? Will I look ridiculous?*

This fear of failure and judgment doesn't just stop us from trying new things; it convinces us to filter our choices through what's "acceptable." We weigh how activities we like will be perceived and avoid the ones that seem silly or unconventional. Real joy doesn't come from permission or approval. It appears when we stop asking *what will people think?* And start asking *what do I love?*

When was the last time you sang out loud without lowering your voice? Danced without being self-conscious? Picked up an old hobby without feeling the need to justify it even to yourself? If you can't remember, maybe it's time to stop letting the fear of embarrassment hold you back. Take the pottery class, even if your mug comes out lopsided. Wear something bold just because it makes you feel good. Dust off that skateboard, that guitar, that long-abandoned passion, not to be great at it, not to impress anyone, but simply because it brings you joy.

Total Presence

Thoughts about the past or worries of the future didn't consume your mind while you played at a young age. If you were playing tag with friends in the park, you weren't overanalyzing something you said earlier or concerned about what was coming tomorrow. Instead, your mind was on the chase and the exhilaration of darting away just in time before being tagged.

Kids are naturally present because they haven't yet developed the habit of multitasking or overthinking. They're fully in the game on the soccer field, running and playing with every ounce of their attention. When building with Legos or setting up scenes with their action figures, they're absorbed in creating, not distracted by what else they could or should be doing.

This ability to immerse yourself entirely in the moment helps make childhood joy feel so intense. Rediscovering how to be this present isn't just a nice idea; it's a game-changer for your mind and body. Being present, or mindfulness helps quiet the noise, pulling you out of the endless loop of past regrets and future worries. A study from *JAMA Internal Medicine* found that practicing mindfulness reduces anxiety and depression. At the same time, research from the American Psychological Association shows it sharpens focus, boosts self-control, and clears mental clutter. It's not just a brain thing. Practicing mindfulness lowers blood pressure, strengthens the immune system, and improves sleep. In a nutshell, being present makes room for happiness.

Intrinsic v. External Motivation

When children put their minds to something, it isn't out of seeking likes, applause, or gold stars. As mentioned above, their joy comes from the activity— the experience of doing, building, imagining, or connecting with their friends. This intrinsic motivation is why kids can spend hours on something without losing interest. They don't chase outcomes or immediate satisfaction; they fuel themselves with the activities that feel the most fun.

But as we move from childhood into adolescence, external validation creeps in. Hormonal shifts, evolving identities, and social pressures turn the spotlight outward. Suddenly, the activity isn't about how much fun it is; it's about whether it will get you noticed. High school sports become more about gaining recognition or status and less about love for the game. How you spend your time outside of school is directly related to what you think will impress your friends, not necessarily what profoundly interests you. The shift from internal to external validation begins, and this is where we stray from the path of true joy.

Moving further into adulthood, external validation cements almost every decision we make. We do things to achieve goals, gain recognition, or fulfill obligations. Maybe you throw yourself into your career, chasing praise from bosses and colleagues, or you make what hobbies you have performance-based, putting pressure on yourself to improve, monetize, or share them publicly. We do this to seek approval from friends, family, and strangers, believing it will bring us happiness. Lasting joy doesn't come from outside sources; it comes from within. It comes from doing things that resonate with who you are, whether or not anyone else sees, cares, or understands.

To rediscover joy, we must reconnect with intrinsic motivation and relearn how to do something for the enjoyment, satisfaction, and personal fulfillment it brings, not because it earns approval. Write a story that no one will read. Paint a picture that will never hang on a gallery wall. Go on a hike for the pleasure of moving your body and being in nature. Do it for you, not for anyone else. The joy you're searching for isn't out there; it's within you.

The *Shoulds*

Perhaps the best thing about being ten is that *shoulds* didn't rule your life. Back then, you didn't worry about spending your time wisely or being productive every moment. You never measured your worth by how much you got done or how impressive your accomplishments were, you simply followed your desires. You climbed trees because it felt thrilling, turned the living room floor into lava because the idea popped into your head, and spent an afternoon building an elaborate domino set up only to watch it tumble. There was no second-guessing or analysis about whether it was a good use of time; it just was.

Then the *shoulds* showed up. Suddenly, we learned a "right way" to spend our time and a "wrong way." We were told we *should* focus on schoolwork instead of flying a kite to ensure we'd be at the top of our class or we *should* play organized sports instead of roller skating because it might earn us a college scholarship. We were told to grow up, get serious, and put childish things aside. Over time, these *shoulds* tightened their grip, and productivity became how we measured our days.

Even when we manage to carry a childhood hobby into adulthood, the pure fun often gets stripped away, replaced by expectations for execution. If you love to paint, you're expected to sell your work; if you love to bake, you're urged to start a side hustle. Free play, simply doing something for the joy of it, gets squeezed out by a culture that values output over experience. The result? We stop permitting ourselves to play. We prioritize what feels worthwhile or useful, even when it leaves us unfulfilled. But joy isn't about utility; it's about doing what feels good, regardless of whether it leads to an achievement, a new skill, or a tangible outcome. The first step to reclaiming joy is taking a break from the *shoulds* and doing something simply because you love it.

REFRAMING JOY AS A NECESSITY

Joy shouldn't be a luxury. It should be more than an optional extra we get to if we have time left after the serious stuff. We shouldn't treat it as a perk, a bonus, or a reward. Joy is foundational; it's a necessity. It's the thread that ties together fulfillment, resilience, and connection. Reclaiming it starts with shifting how we think about happiness and play.

Joy as Fuel, Not a Reward

Adulting is hard. Jobs, bills, relationships, kids, deadlines, the list goes on. We pack our days with obligations, and even when we're not actively working, we carry the overwhelming mental load of keeping everything together. Playing can feel frivolous or even selfish when juggling so many responsibilities. How can you justify spending time reading, learning the newest TikTok dance, or catching up with a friend when there's laundry to do, emails to send, or errands to run? It's no wonder joy often feels like an afterthought, something to get to *if* there's time (and, honestly, there usually isn't).

But the truth is, you can't afford *not* to make time for joy. It revitalizes you, re-energizes you, and reconnects you with who you are beyond the demands of daily life.

Think of joy as the power source for your rechargeable mental battery. Without that source, life starts to feel more difficult. Work becomes draining, relationships feel like a slog, and even the things you're passionate about lose their spark. When you make time for joy, whether it's a five-minute dance break with your daughter, a silly conversation with your bestie, or an hour spent doing something just for you, it recharges that mental battery. It lightens the load. It gives you the energy, creativity, and perspective to keep going.

When you allow yourself to do something just for you, such as doing a crossword puzzle before tackling that challenging email or stepping outside for a quick breath of fresh air in the middle of a packed day, your productivity is enhanced. These small, joyful acts remind you that you're not just a cog in the machine. You're a person who deserves to feel alive and connected every single day.

Play as a Tool for Growth

The word "play" may sound frivolous, something kids do because they don't have responsibilities yet. But play is more than just finding joy, and it's far from trivial. It's one of the most powerful tools for growth, creativity, and connection.

Some of the best ideas come when we're not taking ourselves too seriously and are open to playing with possibilities instead of rigidly sticking to what makes sense. Play creates space for breakthroughs, whether personal, professional, or creative. Take brainstorming sessions, for example. A stiff, overly structured meeting where everyone is afraid to sound foolish rarely sparks innovation. But when you bring in an element of play through improv-style idea generation, thought experiments, or even light competition, you allow people to think beyond the obvious. Pixar, known for its groundbreaking storytelling, encourages employees to intentionally throw out bad ideas, freeing them from the pressure of getting it right on the first try. The result? More unexpected, original ideas that might never have surfaced in a traditional setting.

Play also invites experimentation. Consider an entrepreneur

trying to come up with a new product or service. Instead of sitting down with a spreadsheet and a rigid plan, what if they approached it like a child with a box of LEGOs, testing different configurations, combining ideas that don't seem to fit, and allowing curiosity to lead the way? Many of history's most significant innovations, including Post-it Notes, Velcro, and even the microwave, were the result of experimentation, accidents that turned into game-changing discoveries. When we stop treating work as something that must always be serious and structured, we open ourselves up to creative leaps we never would have reached otherwise. The key is to let go of the notion that play is a distraction and, instead, see it for what it truly is: a tool that helps you become more resilient, innovative, and connected.

Letting Go of Perfection

Perfectionism is one of the most significant barriers to joy. It's that voice in your head saying, "If I'm going to do this, I need to do it right." It's why we hesitate to try new things, abandon hobbies we're not immediately good at, and often feel stuck before we even begin. But joy isn't about getting it right. It's about showing up and enjoying the ride, mistakes and all.

The problem with perfectionism is that it disguises itself as a good thing. It whispers that high standards are what push us forward, that if we just work harder, prepare more, and fine-tune every little detail, we'll finally feel satisfied. But perfection is an impossible finish line. Instead of feeling proud of our progress and what we create, we focus on the flaws. Instead of finding joy in the process, we fixate on the outcome. And if there's even a chance that the result won't be perfect? We procrastinate. We avoid. We become overwhelmed and convince ourselves it's better not to start at all.

This is how perfectionism quietly drains the life out of things that once brought us joy. The simple act of trying, playing, or creating becomes a performance measured against an impossible standard. It turns hobbies into pressure, feedback into criticism, and opportunities into something to be feared. The way back? Loosen the grip. Let yourself be a beginner. Permit yourself to create something messy, to try something new without needing to master it. Perfection was never the point; joy was. And joy is found in *doing*, not in doing it flawlessly.

As a kid, I *loved* to write poems and short stories. I even co-wrote a monthly class newspaper in the 4th grade. I shared my work freely with classmates and family members, with no hesitation and no self-consciousness. I wrote because I enjoyed it, plain and simple. Fast forward to when I first had the idea for this book. Terrifying. Not because I didn't know how to write, but because of that little voice in my head whispering, *What will people think?*

I'm also a die-hard perfectionist. I struggled even to start this book because I expected it to be perfect from the first page. I hesitated to tell friends about it, worried they'd think, *Who does she think she is? Why isn't she doing something more productive, more lucrative?* I had to actively push those judgmental voices out of my head. Whenever I sat down to write or edit, I reminded myself: *Who cares what anyone thinks?* I want to write this. I want to put it out there. If people like it, great. If they don't, oh well.

Self-doubt and seeking external approval can be paralyzing. I felt them constantly throughout this process. But I also knew that if I let them win, this book would never exist. So, I recognized them, shut them down, and kept going. And honestly, that was the biggest victory of all.

CHAPTER 4:
THE SCIENCE OF JOY

Joy isn't just a fleeting, feel-good emotion; it's a superpower. It can transform mental health, deepen relationships, and improve overall well-being. When we tap into joy, we're not just indulging ourselves; we're giving our minds and bodies the boost they need to thrive. I'm not just saying this because it sounds good, science backs it up.

So, let's explore the science behind joy, dive into the brain's chemistry, and unpack the benefits of playful, happy moments. I promise I won't go too deep into it, but it's important to understand how joy, or lack of joy, impacts us physically and mentally.

THE NEUROSCIENCE OF JOY

Let's start with the brain, the control center of everything we experience. When you feel joy, your brain lights up in measurable and powerful ways. It's not just a vague sense of happiness; it's a cascade of chemical reactions that affect how you think, feel, and even heal. Three key players, dopamine, serotonin, and endorphins drive this joyful alchemy.

Dopamine: The Reward Chemical

People often think of dopamine as the 'finish line' chemical, the hit of satisfaction you get when you finally complete a project. But dopamine isn't all about the end result. It's also firing during the process. It's what keeps you engaged, fuels your momentum, and makes the act of doing just as rewarding as being done.

Think about the last time you worked on something you truly enjoyed. Maybe it was painting, piecing together a puzzle, or writing a story. That little spark of excitement when you started? That's dopamine. The satisfaction of solving a problem mid-way through? More dopamine. The tiny thrill of stepping back and seeing progress? Another hit. The brain doesn't wait for you to finish, it rewards you at every step along the way.

This is why creative play feels so good. Whether you're tinkering with a new recipe, designing something just for fun, or testing out a crazy idea at work, your brain is feeding you dopamine, not because you've mastered it, but because you're engaged in it. So, forget the idea that joy only comes when you cross the finish line. Rewards also lie in the *doing*. The trick is to keep moving, keep playing, and let dopamine fuel the process, not just the outcome.

Serotonin: The Mood Stabilizer

If dopamine is the spark of excitement, serotonin is the warm blanket of calm. It's the chemical that helps you feel balanced, at ease, and emotionally steady. While dopamine pushes you to do and achieve, serotonin reminds you to pause and savor.

Serotonin levels naturally rise when you engage in activities that bring you joy. Think about a walk in the woods on a crisp morning, the quiet pleasure of sipping tea while watching the rain, or the contentment of sharing a meaningful conversation with a friend. These moments don't just feel good, they stabilize your mood and create a sense of deep, lasting happiness.

Activities like spending time in nature, meditating, and connecting with others all boost serotonin levels. Joy doesn't always have to be loud or energetic. It can also be quiet, gentle, and restorative.

Endorphins: The Stress Reliever

Ever wonder why a good laugh leaves you feeling lighter or why a brisk walk can melt away the tension of a stressful day? That's endorphins at work. Your body releases endorphins, often called natural painkillers, during physical activity, deep relaxation, and bursts of genuine laughter.

Endorphins help reduce stress and even physical discomfort.

When you engage in movement-based play, like playing frisbee, hiking, or even a game of tag, you're not just having fun; you're giving your body a dose of these powerful stress relievers. Similarly, laughter triggers a rush of endorphins that lift your mood and strengthen your immune system.

The beauty of endorphins is that they're accessible to everyone. You don't need an intense workout or a perfect setting to activate them. You can stretch, go for a walk, share a funny story, or even watch a silly video. Endorphins remind us that joy doesn't have to be elaborate.

JOY AND MENTAL HEALTH

Joy is one of the most effective tools for supporting mental health. Engaging in activities that spark joy assists in regulating emotions, sharpening focus, and developing resilience, creating a foundation for greater well-being. Decades of research have shown that experiencing happiness isn't just about enjoying the good times; it's about building the strength to navigate the hard ones.

Boosting Resilience: Joy as Emotional Armor

Resilience is often described as the ability to bounce back from adversity. It helps us navigate setbacks, losses, and challenges without losing our sense of self. While many factors shape resilience, joy plays a starring role in building this emotional armor.

When you regularly engage in joyful activities, even simple ones, you're training your brain to find balance in difficult times. Think of joy as your emotional home base. When life gets tough, these moments of happiness remind you that not everything is overwhelming or bleak. They anchor you, allowing you to tap into optimism and hope. Consider this: When you were a child, setbacks like hitting the curb with your skateboard or losing a board game didn't crush you. Why? Because your days were filled with small joys that balanced out the challenging moments. The tougher moments take up a smaller percentage of your day, becoming less impactful and less daunting.

Strengthening resilience through joyful activities isn't about avoiding challenges or making them disappear completely; it's about creating the ability to meet them with a steady heart and mind. Joyful habits give you the emotional reserves to weather life's storms and remind you that while hard days are inevitable, so are the moments of lightness that follow.

Micro-joys: Hitting the Stress Reset Button

Stress is an unavoidable part of adult life. Deadlines, responsibilities, and the never-ending to-do list all pile up, triggering our brain to release cortisol, the body's built-in stress alarm. In short bursts, cortisol actually supports focus and alertness. When stress lingers too long, forcing our brain to release this chemical over a more extended period, it drains us, affecting our mood, sleep, and overall well-being. Elevated cortisol levels, often triggered by chronic stress, can disrupt various organ systems by affecting metabolism, suppressing the immune system, and impacting cardiovascular and digestive functions, potentially leading to long-term health issues. Excessive cortisol, often called the "stress hormone," can lead to various health problems when chronically elevated, including weight gain, high blood pressure, weakened immune system, and even increased risk of conditions like Cushing's syndrome.

The good news? Joy is one of the most effective ways to hit reset.

Engaging in playful, joyful activities actively lowers cortisol levels and interrupts stress patterns. Something as simple as laughing, stretching, or humming a favorite song sends a signal to your body: *It's okay to relax.* These small moments of joy, micro-joys, work like pressure-release valves, recalibrating your nervous system before stress takes over. They don't require massive effort or a complete lifestyle overhaul. Just five minutes of doing something lighthearted, watching a funny video, stepping outside for fresh air, or dancing in your kitchen can shift your entire state of mind.

I have a very specific "go-to" micro-joy when I need that extra boost. I work from home, and some days can be stressful. So I take little breaks, just five minutes here and there, to hang out with my dog, Luna. She's always ready for attention and spends most of the day posted up next to my desk, waiting for these mini-breaks.

Sometimes we sit in the backyard and soak up the weather. Other times, we have a quick round of tug-of-war with her favorite dinosaur toy. But most often, I just need a moment to reset, so I give her a few pets, and we "talk" about life (okay, I talk—she listens). She's the perfect companion, always happy with whatever time I can give her. What she doesn't realize is that she's actually giving me more in return.

The more you practice weaving micro-joys into your day, the more your brain learns to seek out these small resets when stress rises. It's like building a mental toolkit for emotional regulation. Try a playlist that instantly lifts your mood, a short walk that clears your mind, or a few deep breaths that bring you back to center. Stress won't disappear overnight, but with regular practice, you start to recalibrate by choosing joy to steady yourself. And that choice, repeated over time, is what builds resilience.

The Science of "Upward Spirals"

Not only does engaging in micro-joys help you reset your stress level, but it also creates what researchers call "upward spirals" of positivity. Actively engaging in positive emotions like joy, gratitude, and hope leads to increased energy, better focus, and stronger relationships. In turn, these benefits open the door to even more opportunities for joy, creating a self-reinforcing cycle of well-being.

Think about the last time you playfully texted back and forth with a friend, memes, and all. That shared moment lifted your spirits at the time and likely made you feel closer to them, too. Strengthening that bond with your friend allows for more of those shared experiences with them, which creates even more opportunities for joy. These upward spirals are the antidote to the downward spirals of stress, where one negative thought or event seems to cascade into another.

By prioritizing joy, you build a foundation for these positive, upward cycles. Not only are you engaging in something that makes you feel good today, but you are also creating a future that allows joy and resilience to feed into each other, lifting you higher with each step.

How to Bring Joy into Your Mental Health Toolkit

Changing your life can feel overwhelming, so when you try to make daily space for positive moments, you might ask, *Where do I start?* You don't need to overhaul your life to reap the mental health benefits of joy. Here are a few simple ways to get started:

1. **Practice Being Present:**

    Pause for a moment. Take a breath. Notice something, anything, that is happening around you. It could be the room's silence, the way sunlight filters through the window, or the comforting warmth of your morning coffee as you sip it. This is being present and recognizing what is unfolding around you. It means letting go of the mental checklist, the future worries, the endless *what's next*, and simply being here, now. When you practice presence, you become more aware of these moments, and over time, your brain starts automatically seeking them out. You begin to enjoy the richness of the present and stop rushing through it. Joy isn't in the next task or accomplishment; it's already here, waiting for you to see it.

2. **Engage in Micro-Joys:**

    Set aside five minutes a day and actively do something fun, whether it's a quick game of Candy Crush, scrolling through photos of your kids on your phone, or working on a Lego build. Take a break and engage in a specific small activity. Enjoy the doing.

3. **Connect with Others:**

    Share your day with friends or family and be involved in theirs as well. Maintaining these connections and building a strong support system amplifies happiness, creating a ripple effect that benefits everyone involved.

4. **Reflect on Joyful Moments:**

   At the end of each day, take a moment to reflect on what brought you happiness. Writing it down can help you notice patterns and prioritize what makes you smile more.

My journey to add micro-joys into my everyday life started with revisiting an old passion. Photography was something I had once loved deeply. I even earned a degree, a Bachelor of Fine Arts, and worked in the field for a while. But as the years passed, I drifted away from it. Life, as it often does, had other plans. A job that paid the bills, raising kids, and managing the everyday chaos of running a household filled my days. Photography quietly slipped to the sidelines. So, when I consciously decided to reintroduce more joy into my life, I thought photography would be a good starting point for a micro-joy. I gave myself a simple challenge: finding five minutes daily to capture something small. Not to create a masterpiece or impress anyone but to find a moment worth noticing and preserving for myself. It could be a newly budding spring flower noticed while walking the dog or the contrast of colors in a pile of laundry. It didn't matter. The only rule was to recognize and snap the shot.

What surprised me was how quickly this simple act reawakened something in me. It reminded me why I'd fallen in love with photography in the first place: the ability to see the world in a new way, to pause and really look. Those fine minute moments sharpened my eye, refocused my mind, and gave me a new appreciation for the ordinary. It felt so natural eventually that "making time" for this micro-joy felt effortless. It felt like a part of my day that I totally looked forward to.

Now, I have a growing collection of photos, a portfolio that's just for me. They're not curated for Instagram or shared with the world. They're a private gallery of joy, each image tied to a specific day, a fleeting feeling, or a moment of beauty I might otherwise have missed. Scrolling through them allows me to reflect on those stolen moments. It's like flipping through a diary, each picture a reminder of the simple, quiet happiness that comes from being present and paying attention to the world around me.

So, I encourage you to consider whether you've left any hobbies or passions in your past. If you have, no matter the reason, consider reigniting that love and making it a starting point, as I did.

CHAPTER 5:
PLAY ISN'T JUST FOR KIDS

At some point, most of us stopped playing. It happens quietly, without fanfare. Life gets serious. Responsibilities pile up and play; the kind that's free, fun, and without purpose is left behind. But the solution to this is simple: all we need to do is redefine what play looks like for us now.

WHAT DOES PLAY LOOK LIKE FOR ADULTS?

We've already discussed the benefits of adult play, but you may be wondering what it actually means to engage in play outside of childhood. Simply stated, play can be anything you do for sheer enjoyment, removing all aspects of competition, goals, or recognition. With this in mind, play can quickly adapt to your current life.

Here are some ways play might show up in adult life:

- **Creative projects:** Drawing, writing, baking, knitting, gardening, or DIY crafts
- **Games:** Board games, card games, video games, or puzzles
- **Exploration:** Trying new activities, visiting unfamiliar places, or learning a new skill
- **Imagination:** Daydreaming, storytelling, or engaging in role-playing games
- **Physical movement:** Hiking, yoga, dancing, or playing a casual game of soccer or frisbee

The possibilities are endless. The only rule is that play should feel lighthearted and fun. If it starts to feel like a chore or an unhealthy competition, it's no longer play; it's work.

BUSTING MYTHS ABOUT PLAY

If you've ever felt like play isn't for you, it could be because of one of the many misconceptions that stopped you from fully embracing the idea. So, let's look at the most popular myths to unlearn what we thought we knew about adult play:

Myth 1: Play Is Unproductive

As touched on earlier, we live in a society that glorifies productivity. If something doesn't lead to a measurable result, money, recognition, or success, it's often seen as a waste of time. But remember, play is incredibly productive in ways that aren't always obvious.

Play helps us recharge so we can approach work and responsibilities with more energy and focus. It fosters creativity, which leads to better problem-solving and innovation. It strengthens our relationships, which are critical for long-term happiness and well-being. In other words, play might be one of the most productive things you can do.

Myth 2: Play Is Silly or Childish

Yes, kids are excellent at play, but that doesn't mean it's only for them. Play is a natural part of being human. It's how we connect with others, explore new ideas, and find joy in the everyday. Far from being childish, play is an act of courage and creativity. It's a way of saying *I value myself enough to give myself the gift of joy.*

Myth 3: I'm Too Busy for Play

This one's tricky because, let's face it, life is busy. But play doesn't have to take hours or involve elaborate plans or special equipment. Play can be as simple as a five-minute stretch break or writing a silly Haiku based on your day. The key is to make space for it, even in small doses. Because the busier you are, the more you need it.

So, to put it simply, play isn't just for kids; it's for anyone who wants to live a happier, more fulfilling life, and that includes you.

THE BENEFITS OF PLAY FOR ADULTS

Throughout the book, we've highlighted the benefits of play for adults. Let's review them now together in the summary below.

1. Play Boosts Creativity

When you're playing, your priority isn't achieving a specific outcome. You're experimenting, exploring, and thinking outside the box, and this is when your brain is at its most creative.

Many of history's greatest thinkers were avid players.

- **Albert Einstein**: Known for his groundbreaking contributions to physics, Einstein often engaged in playful thought experiments, which he referred to as "combinatory play." He believed that this imaginative form of play was essential for creative thinking.

- **Leonardo da Vinci**: A quintessential Renaissance man, his insatiable curiosity and playful experimentation across various disciplines, from art to engineering, were central to his creative genius.

- **Thomas Edison**: With over a thousand patents

to his name, Edison's inventive spirit was fueled by a playful approach to problem-solving, often involving collaborative brainstorming sessions.

I am by no means asking you to become the next Einstein. But by engaging in playful activities in your everyday life, you open yourself up to new ideas and solutions for obstacles you might not have found through traditional methods.

2. Play Reduces Stress

When fully immersed in play, your body releases endorphins, the feel-good hormone that counteracts stress and lowers cortisol levels (the stress hormone). This will help you relax, even after a tough day. Think of it as a mental and emotional reset button.

3. Play Strengthens Relationships

There's something magical about laughing, playing, and sharing joyful experiences with others. Play creates a sense of connection and trust, whether it's through a friendly game of cards, a shared creative project, or simply goofing around with someone you love.

4. Play Improves Work Performance

It might sound counterintuitive, but taking time to play can make you better at your job. Since play boosts creativity, which enhances problem-solving skills and morale, these benefits can also be helpful in your career. Companies like Airbnb, Zappos, and Google have even incorporated play into their workplace cultures with impressive results. Airbnb employees are encouraged to travel, explore, and bring back inspiration. The company also designs its workplace like an adventure, with themed rooms, hammocks, and open spaces that make work feel like an experience, not a chore, when they return to the office. Zappos embraces fun at every level, from costume days to spontaneous office games, knowing that a playful culture leads to happier employees, better ideas, and stronger customer connections. Google takes it even further, turning work into a playground of possibility; nap pods, slides, and creative lounges give employees space to break routine, while their 20% time policy lets them chase passion projects, some of which have changed the world (think Gmail and Google Maps).

5. Play Enhances Emotional Well-Being

Above all, play makes you happier. It reconnects you with the things you love, the people you care about, and the joy of being fully present in the moment. And that's something we could all use more of.

HOW TO REINTRODUCE PLAY INTO YOUR LIFE

If it's been a while since you played, don't worry; it's like riding a bike. Once you start, everything will come back to you naturally. Here are some practical ways to make play a regular part of your life. Pick one or two ideas to start and add the others as you go. This will help this life change feel manageable and not overwhelming.

1. Start Small

You don't need to overhaul your life or dedicate hours to play. Start with a micro-joy, five or ten minutes a day. Try sketching your dog, painting your toenails, or playing catch with a tennis ball against a wall. The goal is to ease into it and let it grow naturally.

2. Try Something New

Play is an excellent opportunity to step outside your comfort zone. If you can carve out more time, consider committing to an activity that will take a little longer, like signing up for a pottery class, an escape room, or joining a local sports league. New experiences spark curiosity and excitement, which are at the heart of play.

3. Bring Play into Your Social Life

As you introduce play back into your life, involve your social circle as much as possible. For example, organize a game night with friends, plan a group outing to a trampoline park, or host a creative workshop. Play is even better when shared, strengthening bonds and creating lasting memories.

4. Make Play Part of Your Routine

Incorporate play into your daily schedule, just like you would with exercise or work. To make this even more doable, combine a playful activity with something you already do or *habit pairing*. This concept, outlined in the Tiny Habits Method created by B.J. Fogg, is simple: you link a new habit to an existing one, making it easier to remember and practice. In this case, it also makes that original task more enjoyable. For example, while brushing your teeth, think of three things you're grateful for.

5. Embrace Physical Play

Movement is a natural form of play, and it's great for both your body and mind. Let's revisit our old friends: dopamine, serotonin, and endorphins. When you move, this powerful trio lifts your spirits, reduces stress, and energizes you. If a gym routine doesn't excite you, find movement that does. Stretch, climb something, chase something, shoot a few hoops. Don't overthink it. Just move. Play. Feel the shift. Your brain and body will thank you.

THE RIPPLE EFFECT OF PLAY

When you prioritize play, the effects ripple into every area of your life. You'll feel more creative, connected, and energized. You'll approach challenges with a fresh perspective and a lighter heart. And you'll rediscover the simple joy that's been waiting for you all along.

I'll end with this: life is serious enough. Play reminds us that joy and creativity are always within reach. All you have to do is make the time to pick up that paintbrush, kick around a soccer ball, or dive into a game with friends.

CHAPTER 6:
RECONNECTING WITH YOUR 10-YEAR-OLD SELF

The last few chapters gave us the foundation: the why, the benefits, and the science behind joy. So now what? How do we take all of that and actually apply it to our real, everyday lives? How do we uncover and live our own recipe for joy?

This is the moment we take that journey back to our childhood to rediscover the ten-year-old version of ourselves who knew how to find joy without hesitation. We will spend some time here, digging deep to recall our younger self. It's not about reliving those days or longing for something that's slipped away. Instead, it's about reconnecting with the essence of who you were when the world felt wide open, your passions burned bright, and you moved through life with an energy that was entirely your own.

This journey isn't a one-size-fits-all adventure. It's personal. It's yours. There's no single path or predetermined map to guide you. It's a process of curiosity and exploration, a chance to uncover the specific moments, activities, and feelings that excited you back then. Each step you take is as unique as the ten-year-old you once were and as present and alive as the person you are now.

GETTING STARTED: UNEARTHING YOUR JOYS

We often bury joy under layers of obligations and expectations, but it patiently waits for us to unearth it. The first step to reviving your childhood passions is remembering what they were. This might sound simple, but it can take some digging, especially if you've spent years immersed in work, family, or other responsibilities.

When I started this exercise, I took the time to step back into my ten-year-old self. I thought about what grade I was in— 4th grade. My teacher? Miss Bruenner. Where did I sit in class? The front (Type A all the way). Best friends? I had three. My favorite color? Purple. How did I like to wear my hair? Always in a ponytail or braids. As I kept going, all these little details about who I was at ten started coming back to me and helped get me back to that time in my life.

Now it's your turn. Close your eyes and imagine yourself at ten. Give yourself some context by visualizing what grade you were in, what you looked like, who your friends were, where you lived, and so on. Take some time to get a complete picture. Write down some key words as you move through the visualization. Once you have a clear picture of the younger you, envision yourself fully absorbed in something you love. What were you doing? Looking through your comic book collection? Conducting a science experiment? Playing a sport? More importantly, how did you feel? Adventurous? Creative? Peaceful? Excited? These emotions are as important as the activities because they made those moments unforgettable.

Once I had the context of my ten-year-old self, I went deeper and focused on what I *loved* to do. Suddenly, it all rushed back: the camping trips, bike riding, the beach, Jump Bands, dance classes, reading, writing, collecting stickers, playing office with my sister, swimming, and even baseball (I was definitely a bit of a tomboy). The list kept growing. There were things I had forgotten entirely about, things I used to get lost in for hours without even thinking about time. I had so much fun reminiscing, slipping back into that younger version of myself who was serious but also a little wild, fearless, and willing to try anything without hesitation. Honestly? I realized I missed her and desperately wanted some of that unbridled joy back.

If you are having trouble stepping back and aren't experiencing that "ah-ha!" moment, here are a few more prompts to help guide you in stepping back:

1. What Did You Lose Track of Time Doing?

Think about the activities that made hours disappear when you were a kid. Maybe it was getting lost in a book under a blanket with a flashlight, weaving friendship bracelets until your fingers ached, or turning the backyard into an obstacle course. Those moments of flow, when time seemed to stand still, are clues to what still has the power to captivate you.

2. What Made You Happiest When No One Was Watching?

Often, what we love most are the things we do purely for ourselves. Maybe you spent hours writing stories you didn't share with anyone, created and operated an imaginary business in your room, or laid on your floor listening to music, gaining inspiration for your own songwriting. Whatever activities you cherished in your private world reveal your unfiltered passions.

3. What Did You Dream About?

Kids are natural dreamers, and our childhood aspirations often reveal what really interests us. Did you dream of being an inventor, an artist, or an explorer? Maybe you imagined opening a bakery, performing on stage, or being a football star. These dreams hold a spark worth revisiting, not as rigid goals but as reminders of the joy and possibility they brought you.

4. What Did You Create?

Childhood is full of making, drawing, building, writing, and imagining. Think about what you created: a model plane, a scrapbook, or a series of wild inventions made from shoeboxes and string. Those creative moments are clues to the kind of activities that can still bring you happiness today.

After working through the memory exercise, I looked at the list I had created and noticed that I had already woven one or two childhood joys into my adult life without even realizing it. One current activity that matched my list was my love of the ocean. As a child, I could spend hours in the water with my brother and sister, boogie boarding, letting the waves carry us into another world. Fast forward to seven years ago when I decided I wanted to learn how to surf. I hadn't been in the ocean for years, but something inside me hadn't forgotten that connection, and I knew it was time to get back in the water. After years of trial and error, I'm now a decent longboarder, and every moment I spend in the water feels like a gift, a direct line back to the joy and freedom I felt at ten.

Some activities on my list surprised me. They were ones I hadn't thought about in decades, and they weren't part of my adult life. Specifically, dancing was the one that stood out the most. Growing up, I'd taken ballet, tap, and jazz lessons up to college. Dancing had been my perfect joy, but as I got older, it faded away, like so many childhood passions do.

Looking at the list, it dawned on me how much I missed it, and I would love to give it a go again. But, finding an adult dance class in my small town proved tricky. So, I got creative.

I started following a few moms on Instagram and TikTok who shared tutorials on shuffling and current dance moves. For fun, I learned a few of the moves. When I remembered how much I enjoyed moving, I took it further and ordered a pair of tap shoes online. Before I knew it, I was in my garage, tapping away to online tutorials, rediscovering the rhythm that had always been a part of me. Even twenty minutes of dancing feels like unlocking a part of myself I'd forgotten, a part that reminds me what it's like to feel alive and playful. And that's the magic of reconnecting with your ten-year-old self; it's not just nostalgia; it's a way back to joy.

Now that you've identified your activities go a little deeper. Reflect on the emotions they stirred. Did building that birdhouse make you feel resourceful and capable? Did writing in your diary with colored pens bring a sense of calm and focus? Did pretending to be an adventurer fill you with excitement and wonder? These feelings are your guide; they're what you're really trying to reconnect with. The exact childhood activity may not fit into your adult life, but developing a new way to evoke that feeling again is the key. Jot down the activity, then write three words that describe how you felt doing it. Are those feelings present in your life today? If not, think of new ways to bring them in. For me, it wasn't about recreating the exact memory of playing in the ocean with my siblings, it was about reclaiming the freedom

I felt in the water. Surfing gave me that. In the same way, maybe you've outgrown reading under a blanket but listening to an audiobook during your commute could offer the same peaceful escape. By focusing on the feeling, you permit yourself to evolve the activity while still honoring its joy.

APPROACH WITH CURIOSITY, NOT JUDGMENT

As you work through this process and take the time to look back at your childhood joys, it's easy to dismiss them. You might think *that was just kid stuff,* or *I've outgrown those things.* But joy doesn't care about age. The activities themselves might have been simple, even silly, but the feelings they evoked? Those are timeless.

When reflecting on what brought you joy at ten, approach it with curiosity. Take the role of detective piecing together clues, not of a critic passing judgment. Be open to whatever comes up, even if it feels insignificant or unrelated to your current life.

For example:

- If you loved playing dress-up, maybe you were drawn to self-expression or storytelling.

- If you spent hours catching bugs or collecting rocks, perhaps the thrill of discovery excited you.

- If you loved building with LEGOs, you might find joy in problem-solving or creating something from scratch.

- If you loved playing a team sport, maybe your happiness lies in game strategy and working with others.

Remember: The goal isn't to replicate your childhood activities exactly; it's to reconnect with the essence of what made them joyful. Was it the freedom to explore? The sense of accomplishment? The way they allowed you to express yourself? These are the threads we're looking for.

BRINGING CHILDHOOD PASSIONS INTO ADULT LIFE

Now that you have your list of activities and evoked emotions, how can you bring those elements into your adult life? Below are a few suggestions to get you thinking.

1. Creativity Without Judgment

If you loved creating art as a kid, try picking it up again, but leave your inner critic at the door. Forget about whether you're good at it or if your work is Instagram-worthy. The point isn't to create a masterpiece; it's to enjoy the process.

- **Try This:** Explore adult coloring books for a relaxing way to ease back into creativity. You can also keep a sketchbook for quick doodling or sign up for a beginner's art class to immerse yourself further.
- **Mindset Shift:** Remember that art doesn't have to be perfect to be meaningful. Creating is valuable, even if no one else ever sees it.

2. Exploring Nature

Remember how magical the outdoors felt when you were a kid? Nature had a way of making the world feel big and full of possibilities. Reconnecting with the natural world as an adult can bring back that sense of wonder.

- **Try This:** Go for a hike, start a small garden, or take a walk in a local park. If you're feeling adventurous, do something new, like paddleboarding or camping.

- **Mindset Shift:** Approach the great outdoors with fresh eyes like you did as a kid. Notice the details: the sound of leaves rustling, the way the sunlight filters through the trees, the patterns on a butterfly's wings.

3. Building or Creating Just for Fun

Building isn't just for kids; it's for anyone who loves the satisfaction of making something with their hands. Creating can be profoundly fulfilling, whether it's woodworking, knitting, or assembling furniture.

- **Try This:** Start a DIY project, build a birdhouse, or learn to bake bread. The key is to choose something that excites you, and you've never attempted before.

- **Mindset Shift:** Focus on the process, not the outcome. It's okay if your project isn't perfect. The joy is in the doing, not the result.

WHAT HAPPENS WHEN YOU RECONNECT

When you reconnect with your ten-year-old memories, you're likely to notice a few things happening:

1. **A Sense of Wholeness:** You'll start to feel more connected to who you are at your core, beyond the roles and responsibilities of adult life.

2. **Renewed Creativity:** Childhood joys often reignite creativity, helping you think outside the box and approach problems with fresh perspectives.

3. **Genuine Happiness:** Focusing on activities that bring intrinsic joy will help you experience deeper and more authentic happiness.

4. **Permission to Play:** Reconnecting with your ten-year-old self permits you to let go of the *shoulds* and loosen up.

As you move forward, remember that this journey isn't about replicating the past but tapping into the unfiltered joy that still lives within you. Let the energy of your ten-year-old self guide you to the activities and emotions that bring you alive. Trust that this process is as unique as you are, and let it remind you that joy is always within reach.

CHAPTER 7: MISSTEPS ON THE ROAD TO JOY

How many times have you purchased something thinking, *This will make me happy*. Maybe you've filled your calendar with exciting plans, convinced that the busier you are, the more fulfilled you'll feel. Let's not forget scrolling through social media, looking for validation in the form of likes and comments.

You're not alone. Many of us fall into these traps while chasing happiness, hoping we can manufacture joy through purchases, packed schedules, or online approval. These things might give us a quick hit of pleasure but rarely lead to lasting joy. Instead, they often leave us feeling emptier, wondering why the happiness we're chasing keeps slipping through our fingers.

Let's examine some of the common missteps on the road to joy and the traps we fall into when we try to shortcut our way to happiness.

TRAP #1: CONSUMERISM: BUYING HAPPINESS

We live in a world that loves to sell us happiness. Ads promise that the right car, the perfect wardrobe, or the latest gadget will make us feel fulfilled. Shopping becomes a quick fix for boredom, stress, or even loneliness. While buying something new can feel good at the moment, that feeling seldom lasts.

Consumerism constantly tells us that joy is something we can acquire, but it's not. You can't buy your way to lasting happiness because joy doesn't come from things; it comes from experiences, connections, and meaning that are unique to you.

Why Buying Doesn't Work

The buzz you get from a new purchase is real, but it's temporary. Psychologists call this the hedonic treadmill: you get a boost of happiness when you acquire something new, but over time, you adapt to it, and the joy fades. That shiny new thing becomes part of the background, leaving you wanting the next new thing. And so on.

We spend so much time, energy, and money chasing possessions that we forget to create moments and experiences that truly matter to our inner selves. It's easy to mistake the thrill of buying for the deeper satisfaction of living a joyful life.

How to Avoid This Trap

- **Pause Before You Purchase:** The next time you feel tempted to buy something, pause and ask yourself: *Am I buying this to solve a problem or because I hope it will make me happy?* If it's the latter, consider participating in one of your five-minute joy exercises, which we discussed in Chapter 4, to avoid the impulse.

- **Invest in Experiences, Not Things:** Research shows that experiences, like a weekend getaway, a cooking class, or a day spent hiking, bring more lasting happiness than material possessions. Experiences create memories, deepen connections, and often lead to stories you'll cherish for years.

- **Find Joy in What You Already Have:** Gratitude is a powerful antidote to consumerism. Take time to appreciate what you already own and the activities you enjoy doing. Use them, enjoy them, and let them remind you that joy doesn't require more stuff.

* Bonus tip: Impulse buying on social media? I've been there, and I've had to work hard to stop it. I found a strategy that works for me. Every time I see something I *have* to buy, instead of clicking "Add to Cart," I copy the link and drop it into a Google Notes list called "Stuff I Want." Then, I close out of the list and tell myself I will revisit it tomorrow. There is no instant purchase, just a cool-off period.

I usually forget that I added something to the list the following day. When I do go back to "Stuff I Want" to take a look, I'm shocked by the things I *thought* I needed. Sometimes, they still resonate, and I will make a purchase. Most of the time, I wonder, *What was I even thinking?* I keep the list intact and don't delete items (unless I purchase them) to remind myself of everything I could have purchased impulsively and didn't need. It's been a game-changer. After a few years of doing this, I've realized that chasing that quick endorphin rush from impulse shopping isn't worth it. I barely use my "Stuff I Want" list anymore, but it's still there in case of an emergency.

TRAP #2: OVER-SCHEDULING: TURNING FUN INTO A TASK

Modern life thrives on busyness; a packed schedule equals success. The more meetings, deadlines, and tasks we juggle, the more important we must be. Busyness has become a status symbol that signals ambition and worth. But when you constantly rush from one thing to the next, you don't necessarily achieve more, you just stay constantly occupied. And yet, we cling to it because busyness gives us a sense of self-importance. It shields us from stillness, from asking the hard questions, *Am I actually happy? Do I even like what I'm doing?*

Why Over-Scheduling Doesn't Work

When you account for every moment of your day, you leave no room for spontaneity, creativity, or rest, and joy needs space to breathe. Even activities you once loved can feel like obligations when crammed into a busy day.

Over-scheduling also leads to burnout. The more we pile onto our plates, the less energy we have to fully enjoy what we're doing. Instead of feeling joyful, we feel drained. Wondering why all our fun plans feel like work.

How to Avoid This Trap

- **Leave Room for Spontaneity:** Block out unstructured time on your calendar. This might feel counterintuitive, but permitting yourself an open, unplanned spot in your day creates space for organic joy. For example, pick a few dates next month and block out a couple of hours each day (or evening). Once your calendar starts to fill, those blocked-out, unstructured times will already be dedicated. When you get to those days, you will have a pleasant surprise of a few hours and the flexibility to do whatever you want: go for a walk, invite a friend for a drink, or see a movie. You create the opportunity to be spontaneous.

- **Say No to Obligations Masquerading as Fun:** Not every invitation or activity deserves a yes. Be intentional about what you commit to, and don't be afraid to protect your time and energy.

- **Focus on Quality, Not Quantity:** Instead of packing your schedule with activities, choose a few that genuinely bring you joy. Give yourself the time and space to savor them rather than rushing from one thing to the next.

Overscheduling, or more so, overcommitting, has been one of my biggest struggles. I am naturally a "yes" person. Need a chaperone for the field trip? I'm in. Looking for a team mom? Sign me up. Need a Chairperson for the annual school fundraiser? Yep, I'll do it. I always said yes because I loved to help, but at some point, I had to ask myself, was I doing it for the right reasons? Was I really finding that much fulfillment in these things, or was I trying to prove how helpful I was, feel needed, or get validation? I'm still not sure.

What I *do* know is that all those yeses led to plain chaos, juggling work, kids, and too many commitments. I wasn't productive and simply ran myself into the ground. A few years ago, a text convo with a friend changed everything. She pointed out something so simple: *I could just stop saying yes. I could choose myself by saying no.* For some reason, her simple insight resonated with me. At first, it felt selfish to say no, but I soon realized it was self-preservation.

Since then, I've learned that saying no to what may drain me means I have more space to say yes to the things that actually bring me joy. And honestly? That shift has made me a better person, a better partner, and a better mom.

TRAP #3: SOCIAL MEDIA: MISTAKING LIKES FOR CONNECTION

Social media is a double-edged sword. On one hand, it's a tool for staying connected and sharing moments of joy. On the other hand, it can quickly become a source for validation-seeking and superficial interactions. The likes, comments, and followers we talked about earlier might feel good, but they're no substitute for actual, meaningful connections.

Why Social Media Doesn't Work

Social media often creates the illusion of connection without delivering the real thing. It's easy to mistake a like for genuine support or a comment for a meaningful conversation. But scrolling through highlight reels and curated feeds can leave us feeling disconnected and more alone than ever. Researchers have linked curated feeds on platforms like Instagram to increased anxiety, depression symptoms, feelings of inadequacy, and fear of missing out.

Social media also distracts us from the present. Instead of thoroughly enjoying a moment, we focus on capturing it, posting it, and waiting for others to validate it. In the process, we miss the chance to be present and allow the joy and validation we seek to come from within.

How to Avoid This Trap

- **Be Intentional About Your Time Online:** Set

boundaries for how and when you use social media. For example, limit your scrolling to a specific time of day or take breaks when you notice it's making you feel anxious or drained. A 2022 study published in *Science Daily* showed that limiting social media interaction to 30 minutes a day leads to lower levels of anxiety, depression, loneliness, and trouble sleeping.

- **Focus on Real-Life Connections:** Put the phone down and make a point to nurture your offline relationships. Schedule lunch dates, call a friend, or spend quality time with loved ones. These connections are far more fulfilling than anything in your feed.

- **Share for the Right Reasons:** If you enjoy sharing moments of your life online, do it for yourself, not for likes or approval. Post things that bring you joy, and let go of the need for external validation. I don't post a lot on social media. I'm more of a lurker, scrolling and seeing what everyone else is up to. But I fully understand the rush that comes from posting something and getting a wave of likes. When I *do* post, I notice my behavior shifts. I start checking Instagram constantly to see who's liking and commenting. And yes, it feels good when I get a lot of traction, but after about a day, the excitement fades, and I move on.

I can see how easy it is to get hooked and how the quick hit of validation can lead to more and more posting, turning Instagram into a constant search for attention. It's not realistic for me to say, *stop opening Instagram*. But if you enjoy sharing and don't want to get caught up in the like/comment cycle, I like the idea of turning off the likes and comments on your posts. That way, you can still share what you love without the pressure of external validation. Give it a shot; you might be surprised by how freeing it feels.

FINDING JOY WITHIN

The common thread in all these traps is the belief that joy comes from the outside. But real joy doesn't live in what's purchased or posted. It lives in what's felt. It's not something you acquire; it's something you cultivate. That doesn't mean you must reject modern pleasures or stop sharing your life altogether. It simply means shifting your focus inward. Before you chase the next shiny thing or add another event to your calendar, pause and ask yourself: *What does authentic joy look like for me? Am I doing this for myself or someone else's approval?* When you approach joy with curiosity and intention, you'll see that it's never been as out of reach as it sometimes feels. Because at the end of the day, joy isn't about what you own, the plans you make, or the likes you get. It's about finding meaning, connection, and wonder in the life you're already living. And that's something no trap can take away from you.

CHAPTER 8: MAKING JOY A HABIT

So far, we've explored what individual joy truly means, those moments of genuine happiness, free of judgment or obligation, and the missteps we sometimes take trying to recreate it as adults. We've pinpointed how what you loved to do at ten was less about the specific activity and more about the emotions it stirred. Maybe the exact activities don't slot neatly into your current life (though if they do, that's a bonus), but the feelings they evoked can be revived in new and meaningful ways.

We've also explored the idea of turning to micro joys, these 5-minute emergency breaks to employ as a way to relieve stress or reset during the day. What if you took it a bit further than a few impromptu breaks and actually created an intentional joy routine? This practice would work in parallel with your daily schedule and, with enough practice, become a habit.

The idea of making joy a habit might sound strange at first. Isn't joy supposed to be spontaneous, unplanned, and free-flowing? Yes and no. While it's true that joy often arises naturally, creating an environment for it to grow ensures you're not relying on chance to feel happy. You can prioritize happiness by building joy into your day, even when life feels hectic. And the best part? The more you practice, the more joy becomes second nature.

CREATING JOYFUL ROUTINES

Habits thrive on consistency and ease. To make joy a habit, you'll need a game plan. The goal is to create routines that naturally incorporate joy into your day without having to put maximum effort into making it happen. Here are some practical ways to get started:

1. Morning Rituals for Joy

How you start your day matters. A joyful morning routine sets the tone for the hours ahead, helping you approach your day with curiosity and positivity.

Ideas for a Joyful Morning:

- Spend an extra five minutes in bed before you get up, visualizing the day ahead, and then journal what part of your day you're looking forward to.
- As your coffee is brewing, go outside, even for a moment, to feel the fresh air and connect with nature.

- Play music that energizes or inspires you while you get ready.
- While your breakfast cooks, do something physical like stretching to wake up your body and mind

The key is to choose an activity that feels natural and enjoyable, not forced. Ultimately, the ritual(s) you include in your morning should make you smile and not jeopardize your schedule.

As for me, I love lists. So, each morning, over coffee, I spend no more than ten minutes updating my "To Do Today" list and my "Joys For Today" list. The "To Do" list is practical, a brain dump of everything that needs to get done. The "Joys" list is intentional, a plan for weaving happiness into the day. If grocery shopping is on my To Do list, my Joys list might include picking up treats for a sundae bar. The thought of making sundaes with my family after dinner makes the chore feel lighter. This simple practice brings order and anticipation to my day, setting the tone for balance and delight. If lists aren't your thing, keep thinking! It may take some trial and error to find a morning routine that speaks to you, but you'll find it.

2. Habit Pairing Throughout the Day

As discussed in Chapter 5, habit pairing is a fantastic tool for adding moments of joy to your life. It is a game-changer when it comes to building joy into your routine.

Suggestions for Daily Habit Pairing:

- While you catch up on the latest Netflix show, do five minutes of stretching to relax
- As you check your email, play a favorite song
- When tidying up around the house, listen to a podcast
- Long commute to work and back? Call a friend to catch up (hands-free, of course)

By anchoring joy to something you're already doing (that may feel like a grind), the job becomes less heavy and might even put a smile on your face.

I'm the designated dog walker in the family. Most days, I enjoy it; some days, it's just another chore on an already-packed to-do list. But I've found a simple way to shift my mindset: I always pop on a podcast or audiobook as I walk. On busy days especially, this turns what feels like an obligation into 30 minutes of "me time." The dog still gets the walk, but I get something even better: a moment that's mine.

3. Evening Wind-Down Rituals

Evenings are a time to unwind, reflect, and recharge, so creating an evening ritual centered around joy is just as important as it is in the morning.

Ideas for a Joyful Evening:

- Write down one thing that brought you joy during the day
- Read a few pages of a book
- Engage in a creative hobby like learning calligraphy
- Take a warm bath with a favorite scent and let yourself relax

Reflecting on what went well during the day reinforces the habit of noticing joy, so evening rituals are an excellent opportunity to practice gratitude.

FLEXIBILITY IS KEY

Life events have a way of messing with routines, and that's okay. The goal of building joy into your day isn't to force a rigid system; it's to create a flexible one. If you miss a day of infusing joy or need to adapt your routine, don't worry.

Adapting to Life's Changes
- **Busy Days:** On particularly hectic days, aim for one micro-joy. Maybe it's a two-minute stretch or a quick message to a friend.
- **Changing Seasons:** Your routines might need to shift as the seasons change. In the summer, joy might look like an evening walk; in the winter, it might be curling up with a blanket and a hot drink. Stay open to what the day offers you.

- **Energy Levels:** Some days, you'll feel ready to tackle a big project or try a new local community class. On other days, you'll want to rest. Honor your energy and adjust your routines accordingly.

TRACKING YOUR JOY

One of the best ways to reinforce the habit of joy is to track it. By recording your joyful moments, you'll notice patterns, preferences, and the small things that consistently make you happy. Plus, reflecting on your joy can be a joyful experience in itself.

How to Track Joy

- **Journaling:** Keep a notebook or digital journal where you jot down at least one joyful moment each day. For inspiration, focus on what makes you smile or feel content.

- **A Joy Jar:** Write down your happy moments on slips of paper and place them in a jar. Over time, you'll have a visual reminder of all the good in your life. To seamlessly incorporate this tracker into your life, consider adding to the Joy Jar as part of your evening routine.

- **Photo Diaries:** Take a picture of something that brings you joy each day. It could be a beautiful view, a favorite meal, or a playful moment with a friend. My five-minute daily photo micro-joy, which I discussed in Chapter 4, has created an amazing photo diary, and I love it.

Tracking joy doesn't need to be time-consuming. Even a simple mental note at the end of the day can help you stay mindful of the happiness you're creating. Remember, the goal isn't to fill every moment with happiness; it's to make space for joy to thrive. So go ahead. Start small, stay flexible, and let joy become a habit that lasts a lifetime.

CHAPTER 9: THE JOY OF CONNECTION

We often think of joy as something personal, an internal state to be nurtured and protected. While that's true, it's only part of the picture. Joy is also communal. It thrives in connection, relationships, and moments that bring us closer to one another. When you make joy a habit, something magical happens: it ripples outward. The small moments of happiness you create for yourself can influence the people around you. You might find that your playful energy sparks laughter in your family or that your gratitude inspires a friend to reflect on their own blessings. Joy has this amazing ability to multiply when it's shared. Whether it's an inside joke, a collaborative project, or simply a moment of connection, joy strengthens our bonds with others and reminds us that we're all in this together.

Let's explore the power of shared joy and how joy can transform your life and the lives of those around you.

WHY SHARED JOY MATTERS

Humans are hardwired for connection. *Harvard Health Publishing* reports that our brains respond positively to social interaction and that meaningful relationships are one of the biggest predictors of long-term happiness. As mentioned earlier, when we share joy with others, we're not just creating a happy moment; we're strengthening relationships, building trust, and fostering a sense of belonging. In today's often disconnected world, that's more important than ever.

When we experience joy with others, our brains release oxytocin, the bonding hormone. This chemical helps us feel closer to those we're with, creating a sense of connection and trust. At the same time, laughter and play activate our body's natural stress relievers, as we learned earlier. This lowers our cortisol levels and makes us feel more relaxed and open.

In a study published in *PLOS ONE* in 2019, researchers found that shared positive experiences were more impactful on long-term well-being than solitary ones. It's not just about feeling good; it's about feeling good *together*.

Shared joy can also be a powerful way to bridge differences and foster understanding. Playing together reminds us of our shared humanity. In those moments, labels, roles, and differences fall away, and we connect on a deeper level. Joy creates a space where everyone belongs and can be our most original selves.

WAYS TO SHARE JOY

So, how do we bring more shared joy into our lives? It starts with intention. Building joyful connections doesn't have to be complicated or time-consuming. Conceive simple ways to come together and create moments of meaning. Use your list of activities you enjoyed at age ten to work from. For example:

1. Host a Game Night

Maybe you loved to play board games when you were young. There's a good chance others did too. Why not gather friends and/or family members and share the experience? There's something timeless about gathering around a table with snacks and a board game. Game nights are an easy and accessible way to bring people together, and they're a great reminder that play isn't just for kids.

- **What You'll Need:** A few favorite games, a comfortable space, and maybe some snacks or drinks to set the mood.
- **Tips for Success:** Choose games that are easy to learn and inclusive. Think party games, trivia, or collaborative games where everyone works together toward a common goal.

- **Why It Works:** Games encourage teamwork and a bit of friendly competition. Both of which are perfect for building connections.

2. Create Together

If being creative was your thing when you were a kid, invite friends and/or family members over and host a creative casual evening. Creativity breaks down social barriers by fostering collaboration, promoting empathy, and creating shared experiences that transcend differences. It sparks joy by encouraging authentic expression, playfulness, and connection, making people feel more united and alive. Whether crafting or cooking, collaborative creative activities allow you to share ideas, learn from one another, and create something meaningful together.

- **What You'll Need:** Basic supplies like paper, colored pencils or pens, or a recipe & ingredients. You don't need anything fancy, keep it simple and accessible.

- **Ideas to Try:** Host an art night where everyone works on their masterpiece, or cook a meal together and enjoy the fruits of your labor. If you're feeling ambitious, try a group project like building a community mural or planting a garden.

- **Why It Works:** Creating together taps into our innate need to express ourselves, and doing it in a group setting amplifies the joy.

3. Get Outside

Nature has a way of bringing people together, whether it's through a hike, a picnic, or a community cleanup. Outdoor activities are a chance to connect not just with others but also with the world around you.

- **What You'll Need:** A bit of planning, comfortable shoes, and a sense of adventure.
- **Ideas to Try:** Coordinate a group hike, plan a picnic in the park, or join a local gardening project. If you're feeling playful, set up an outdoor scavenger hunt or organize a game of frisbee.
- **Why It Works:** Being outside encourages movement, curiosity, and mindfulness, all of which enhance our ability to connect and share joy.

4. Celebrate Just Because

Why wait for a birthday or holiday to throw a party? Sometimes, the best celebrations are the ones that don't have a reason. Gather your friends, pick a theme (or don't), and simply enjoy being together.

- **What You'll Need:** A welcoming space and an open invitation.
- **Ideas to Try:** Host a potluck dinner or a "throwback" party with music and games from your childhood, or plan a small gathering where everyone shares a story or talent.

- **Why It Works:** Celebrations remind us to slow down and appreciate the people around us. They create moments of shared joy that linger long after the party ends.

BUILDING YOUR JOYFUL CIRCLE

Creating a community of joy doesn't happen overnight, but it begins with simple, intentional steps. Here are some tips for building your circle of connection:

- **Start Small:** You don't need a huge group to experience the joy of connection. Start with a couple of close friends or family members. Focus on quality over quantity.
- **Be the Initiator:** Sometimes, people hesitate to set up events because they're worried no one will come. The truth is, most people crave connection. They need someone to take the first step. Be that person.
- **Focus on Shared Interests:** Think about the activities that bring you joy and invite others to join you. Shared interests, such as basketball, crafting, or card games, create a natural foundation for connection.
- **Embrace Imperfection:** Not every gathering will be perfect, and that's okay. The point isn't to create a flawless gathering; it's to create a space for connecting.
- **Make It Regular:** Consistency is key to building a joyful community. Regular gatherings, such as a weekly

walk, a bi-monthly book club, or a monthly game night, create a sense of rhythm and belonging.

Two years ago, I started a hiking group to reconnect with my community of friends and my love for the outdoors. Growing up, my family didn't take extravagant vacations. We went camping. Those trips were filled with hiking, fishing, and exploring the wild. When I made my list of childhood joys, camping was another activity that stood out. While pitching a tent isn't practical in my everyday life, I realized it wasn't about the camping itself but about being outdoors and exploring. Hiking was the perfect way to bring that joy into my adult life, and living in an area with plenty of trails made it easy to start.

At first, I hiked alone and loved it. I couldn't shake the idea that it would be even better with friends. So, I created a text group of about 20 women I thought might enjoy regular hikes and gave our group a fun name: *Mother Trekkers*. The response was incredible, and to this day, every Thursday after morning school drop-off, we meet at a different local trail. There are no rules, come when you can, skip when you can't. Some weeks, one person shows up. Other weeks, it's a crew of ten. No matter the turnout, the jokes, conversations, and connection we share on the trail have become irreplaceable. Starting this group has brought joy to me and everyone who's joined. *Mother Trekkers* has become one of the highlights of my week.

CHAPTER 10: LIVING A LIFE GUIDED BY JOY

Looking back on these pages, we've traveled quite a journey together. From the carefree days of being ten to the complexity of adult life, we've examined how joy can slip through our fingers and, more importantly, learned how to reclaim it. This journey has shown us that joy is not a reward waiting at the end of the road, but the road itself. It's a way to move through life that makes everything a little lighter, more colorful, and a lot more meaningful.

I urge you to take these lessons, stories, and strategies and turn them into something lasting. Joy isn't just a feeling; it's a choice, a practice, and a mindset. When you choose to live a life guided by joy, you're making a commitment to yourself to honor what lights you up, embrace what makes you feel alive, and live in an authentic and true way.

Let's reflect, look back at what we've uncovered, and see how far we've come. Then, let's look forward to a life where joy isn't an occasional visitor but a constant companion.

THE JOURNEY BACK TO TEN

Ten-year-old you. The one who jumped rope, doodled castles, or raced their bike until their legs burned. That version of you had an uncanny ability to find joy in the simplest things. It wasn't something you planned or scheduled; it was something you lived. You followed what felt good, what sparked curiosity, what made you laugh until your sides hurt.

As we've explored, growing up often means leaving that effortless joy behind. The world tells us we must be serious, productive, and purposeful. We internalize the idea that joy is something we earn, not something we're entitled to. Before we know it, our days are filled with obligations, our minds with expectations, and our hearts with longing for something we can't quite name.

Yet, that ten-year-old version of you hasn't gone anywhere. They're still there, tucked away beneath the layers of adult life. They're not mad at you for getting caught up in the hustle. They just want you to remember what it's like to be free, to play, to create, to be unapologetically you. They're waiting patiently.

WHAT HAPPENS WHEN JOY TAKES THE LEAD

When we prioritize joy, something shifts inside of us. Life feels less like a series of checkboxes and more like an adventure. We start to see possibilities where we once saw limits, to find meaning in the mundane, and to connect more deeply with ourselves and others. Joy doesn't eliminate life's challenges; it gives us the resilience to face them. It doesn't solve our problems; it changes how we approach them.

Authenticity Takes Center Stage

Joy has a way of stripping away the noise. When you follow what brings you joy, you're guided by your inner compass, not by what society, your boss, or your friends think you should be doing. You make choices that align with your values, passions, and unique spirit. In doing so, you become the most accurate version of yourself.

Balance Becomes Possible

A life guided by joy isn't about ignoring responsibilities or avoiding hard work. It's about creating balance, making space for what nourishes you alongside the things that demand your attention. When you prioritize joy, you're not escaping life but enhancing it. You're reminding yourself that your well-being is as important as your to-do list.

Joy Becomes Contagious

One of the most beautiful things about living joyfully is that it is infectious. It doesn't just change your life; it changes the lives of those around you. When you play and embrace life with openness, you invite others to do the same. You strengthen relationships, build connections, and create a ripple effect of happiness that extends far beyond you.

JOY AS A WAY OF BEING

Joy is not a place you arrive after you've done everything right. It's not the result of a perfect plan or a flawless life. It's a choice you make every day, in small ways, repeatedly.

Living a life guided by joy doesn't mean you'll never be sad, stressed, or overwhelmed. It doesn't mean you'll always have time for play or never fall into old patterns. It means you commit to returning to joy, even when it feels far away. It means you give yourself permission to seek happiness, even when the world gets heavy. And it means you trust that joy is always within reach, even in the simplest, smallest moments.

A CHALLENGE FOR THE JOURNEY AHEAD

As we wrap up this journey, I want to leave you with a challenge. It's simple, but it's powerful: every day, do one thing that would make your ten-year-old self smile.

It doesn't have to be big or elaborate. Maybe it's walking through the grass barefoot or eating your favorite childhood snack. Perhaps it's calling a friend to laugh about something ridiculous or building a pillow fort with your kids. Whatever it is, let it be something that reminds you of that carefree, curious, joyful spirit you once were and still are.

This isn't just a fun exercise (though it's definitely that). It's a way to practice choosing joy, even when life gets busy or complicated. It's a way to reconnect with the parts of yourself that are playful, creative, and alive. And it's a way to remind yourself, every single day, that happiness isn't a luxury; it's a priority.

REMINDERS FOR STAYING CONNECTED TO JOY

To help you stay on track, here are a few reminders for making joy a regular part of your life:

Start Small

You don't need to overhaul your life to prioritize joy. Begin with micro-joys, those tiny, fleeting moments of happiness. Over time, these small acts add up to something much bigger.

Reflect Regularly

Set aside some time at the end of each day, or at the very least, at the end of each week to reflect on what brought you joy. What worked? What didn't? What surprised you? By staying curious and open, you'll learn more about what truly makes you happy.

Be Flexible

Life is unpredictable, and so is joy. Some days, your joyful moment might be working on a detailed do-it-yourself home project; other days, it might be a quiet cup of tea. Let go of perfectionism and allow joy to take whatever form it needs.

Share Your Joy

Happiness is meant to be shared. Invite others to join you in playful activities, talk about what makes you happy, or simply smile at a stranger. When you share joy, you multiply it.

Keep Your Ten-Year-Old Self Close

When in doubt, ask yourself: What would ten-year-old me do? Let that younger version of you guide your decisions, inspire your creativity, and remind you to have a little fun along the way.

A LIFE WELL-LIVED

At its heart, *Now & Ten* is about reclaiming the joy that's always been yours. The happiness you felt at ten wasn't a fluke; it was a glimpse of what life could be when you're free to follow your heart, your curiosity, and your delight. Now that you know that joy is still within you, it's time to nurture it.

As you move forward, let joy be your compass. Let it guide your choices, shape your days, and remind you who you are. And remember: a joyful life isn't a perfect life; it's an authentic one. It's a life where you make space for what matters, embrace the messy, beautiful journey, and give yourself permission to play, explore, and be.

So go ahead. Jump on the bike. Turn up the music. Chase the dream. Most of all, commit to doing one thing each day that makes your ten-year-old self smile because that's the kind of life you deserve: one filled with light, laughter, and a little bit of magic.

www.ingramcontent.com/pod-product-compliance
Lightning Source LLC
Chambersburg PA
CBHW050917160426
43194CB00011B/2440